Getting Along with Others

An Activity Book

Author: Ron Herron
Illustrator: David Lee Ronk

BOYS TOWN℠
Press

Boys Town, Nebraska

Getting Along With Others

Published by The Boys Town Press
Father Flanagan's Boys' Home
Boys Town, Nebraska 68010

Copyright © 1996 by Father Flanagan's Boys' Home

ISBN-10: 0-938510-98-3
ISBN-13: 978-0-938510-98-7

Boys Town Press is the publishing division of Boys Town, a national organization serving children and families.

For a free Boys Town Press catalog, call 1-800-282-6657
Visit our web site at www.boystownpress.org

Boys Town National Hotline
1-800-448-3000
Kids and parents can call toll-free, anytime, with any problem.

10 9 8 7 6 5 4

Using a Quiet Voice

1. Listen to your voice.
2. If your voice is loud, make it quieter.

Name: _____

My Reward: _____

_____

_____

Asking for Help

1. Decide what you need help with.

2. Decide who can help you.

3. Look at the person when you ask for help.

4. Say "Please" and "Thank you."

Name: _____

My Reward: _____

_____

_____

Sharing Your Feelings

1. Look at the person.

2. Use a quiet voice.

3. Tell the person how you feel and why.

  ("I feel _____ because_____")

Name: _____

My Reward: _____

_____

Following Instructions

1. Look at the person.
2. Say "Okay."
3. Do what was asked.
4. Check back.

Name: _____

My Reward: _____

_____

4

Letting People Know Where You Are

1. Tell whoever is taking care of you where you're going.

2. Be sure you go there.

3. Check in with the person when you come back.

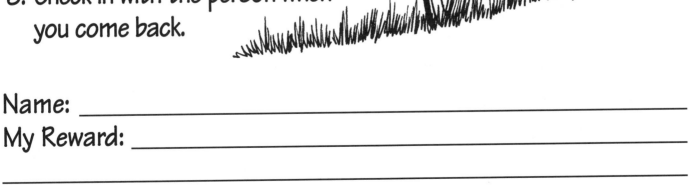

Name: _____

My Reward: _____

_____

_____

5

Saying Something Nice

1. Decide what you want to say.

2. Look at the person.

3. Use a quiet voice and smile.

4. Say what you like about the other person.

Name: _____

My Reward: _____

_____

Getting Someone's Attention

1. Look at the person.
2. Ask the person to watch you or listen to you.
3. Just ask once and then wait.
4. Thank the person for watching or listening.

Name: _____

My Reward: _____

_____

_____

7

Saying You're Sorry

1. Think of what you are going to say.
2. Look at the person.
3. Say "I'm sorry."
4. Tell the person what you did wrong.

Name: _____

My Reward: _____

_____

_____

Solving Problems on Your Own

1. Think of three ways to solve the problem.

2. Think of what is good and bad about each one.

3. Pick the one you think is best and try it.

4. If you get stuck, ask for help.

Name: _____

My Reward: _____

_____

9

Picking Up After Yourself

1. Pick up your things without being asked.

2. Put your toys and clothes where they belong.

3. Tell Mom or Dad what you have done.

Name: _____

My Reward: _____

_____

10

Disagreeing in a Nice Way

1. Listen to the other person.
2. Use a quiet voice and say why you disagree.
3. Think about what the other person says.
4. Respect the person's right to disagree with you.

Name: _____

My Reward: _____

_____

_____

11

Offering to Help Someone

1. Notice when someone is having a hard time.

2. Look at the person.

3. Ask if you can help.

Name: _____

My Reward: _____

_____

Thanking Someone

1. Notice when someone does something nice for you.

2. Look at the person and smile.

3. Say "Thank you" and tell them what you liked.

Name: _____

My Reward: _____

_____

_____

Using Good Table Manners

1. Sit still and use a quiet voice.
2. Use your napkin and silverware.
3. Chew with your mouth closed.
4. Talk only when your mouth is empty.

Name: _____

My Reward: _____

_____

_____

Making a New Friend

1. Look at the other person.
2. Say "Hi" or "Hello."
3. Tell the person your name.
4. Ask for that person's name.
5. Ask the person to play.

Name: _____

My Reward: _____

_____

Sharing Things with Others

1. Don't get upset if you're asked to share.

2. Take turns and play fair.

3. If the person thanks you, say "You're welcome."

Name: _____

My Reward: _____

_____

_____

Listening to Others

1. Look at the person who is talking.
2. Think about what is being said.
3. Don't interrupt.

Name: _____

My Reward: _____

_____

_____

Telling the Truth

1. Look at the person.
2. Say exactly what happened.
3. Answer any questions honestly.

Name: _____

My Reward: _____

_____

Showing You Care

1. Look at the person.
2. Say something nice.
3. Help the person if you can.

Name: _____

My Reward: _____

_____

_____

19

Accepting 'No'

1. Look at the person.
2. Say "Okay."
3. Don't argue.

Name: _____

My Reward: _____

_____

_____

Interrupting in a Nice Way

1. Look at the person.

2. Wait for the other person to respond.

3. Follow instructions from that person.

4. Tell the person why you interrupted.

Name: _____

My Reward: _____

_____

_____

Asking Permission to Do Something

1. Look at the person.
2. Say "Please," or "May I…."
3. Ask for what you want.
4. Say "Thank you."

Name: _____

My Reward: _____

_____

_____

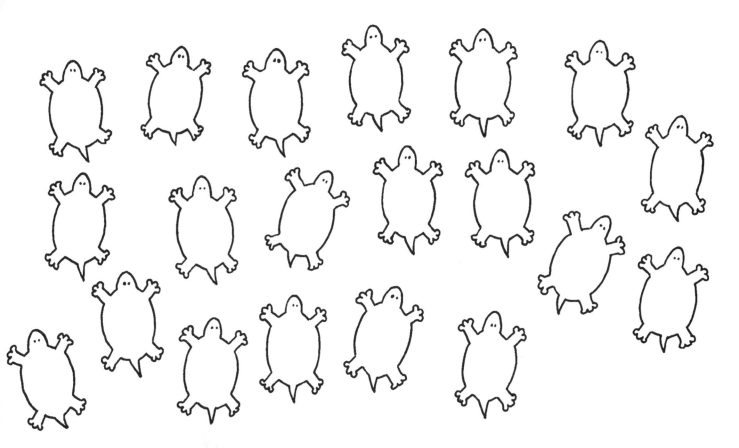

Controlling Your Anger

1. Take a deep breath.
2. Don't hit, yell, or throw things.
3. Tell yourself to calm down.
4. If possible, go to a quiet place.

Name: _____

My Reward: _____

_____

_____

Correcting Mistakes

1. Look at the person.
2. Listen to what you did wrong.
3. Say "Okay."
4. If possible, do it over the right way.

Name: _____

My Reward: _____

_____

_____

Skill: _____

Steps 1. _____
2. _____
3. _____
4. _____

Name: _____

My Reward: _____

_____

Skill: _____

Steps
1. _____
2. _____
3. _____
4. _____

Name: _____

My Reward: _____

_____

_____

Skill: _____

Steps
1. _____
2. _____
3. _____
4. _____

Name: _____

My Reward: _____

_____

_____

Skill: _____

Steps
1. _____
2. _____
3. _____
4. _____

Name: _____

My Reward: _____

_____

Skill: _____

Steps 1. _____

2. _____

3. _____

4. _____

Name: _____

My Reward: _____

_____

_____

Skill: _____

Steps 1. _____
      2. _____
      3. _____
      4. _____

Name: _____

My Reward: _____

_____

30